Afraid

Julie Murray

Abdo
EMOTIONS
Kids

abdopublishing.com

Published by Abdo Kids, a division of ABDO, PO Box 398166, Minneapolis, Minnesota 55439.
Copyright © 2017 by Abdo Consulting Group, Inc. International copyrights reserved in all countries.
No part of this book may be reproduced in any form without written permission from the publisher.

Printed in the United States of America, North Mankato, Minnesota.

052016

092016

 THIS BOOK CONTAINS
RECYCLED MATERIALS

Photo Credits: AP Images, iStock, Shutterstock

Production Contributors: Teddy Borth, Jennie Forsberg, Grace Hansen

Design Contributors: Christina Doffing, Candice Keimig, Dorothy Toth

Cataloging-in-Publication Data

Names: Murray, Julie, author.

Title: Afraid / by Julie Murray.

Description: Minneapolis, MN : Abdo Kids, [2017] | Series: Emotions | Includes
    bibliographical references and index.

Identifiers: LCCN 2015959123 | ISBN 9781680805215 (lib. bdg.) |
    ISBN 9781680805772 (ebook) | ISBN 9781680806335 (Read-to-me ebook)

Subjects: LCSH: Fear--Juvenile literature. | Emotions--Juvenile literature.

Classification: DDC 152.5/6--dc23

LC record available at http://lccn.loc.gov/2015959123

Table of Contents

Afraid

We feel **uneasy** when we are afraid. It is an **emotion**.

Gus is lost. He is afraid.

Another word for afraid
is scared.

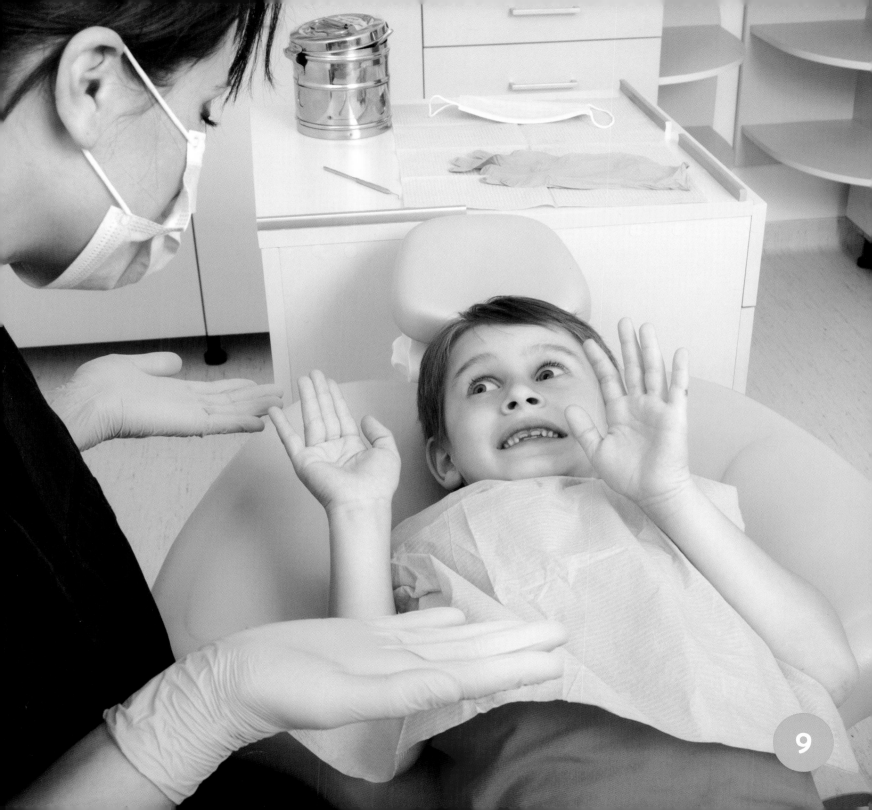

Abby hugs her teddy bear.

She is afraid of the dark.

11

Kim watches a movie.

It is scary. She feels afraid.

Max hears a loud noise.

He is afraid.

Jake doesn't want to jump.

He is afraid of heights.

Tim sees a bee. He got stung when he was little. Now he is afraid of bees.

When have you felt afraid?

21

Things to Do When We Are Afraid

draw what you're afraid
of and rip it up

learn about what
scares you

face your fear with
friends or family

think of your favorite
happy moment

Glossary

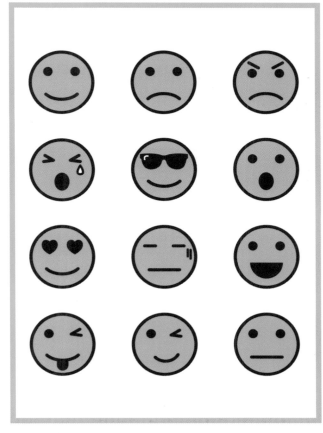

emotion
a strong feeling.

uneasy
worried or uncomfortable.

Index

abdokids.com

Use this code to log on to abdokids.com and access crafts, games, videos, and more!

Abdo Kids Code:
EAK5215

24